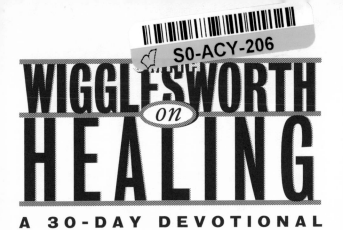

WIGGLESWORTH *on* HEALING

A 30-DAY DEVOTIONAL

Thanks for believing —
continuing to believe —
we love you —
Mmy & Egne

Edited and Compiled by
Larry Keefauver

Charisma
HOUSE
A STRANG COMPANY

Smith Wigglesworth on Healing
by Larry Keefauver
Published by Charisma House
A Strang Company
600 Rinehart Road
Lake Mary, FL 32746
www.charismahouse.com

All Scripture quotations are from
the King James Version of the Bible.

Library of Congress Catalog Card
Number: 96-84888
International Standard Book
Number: 0-88419-438-8

A word about the cover:
The writing in the background is the actual
handwritten letter that Smith Wigglesworth
started the day before he died. His letter shares
the details of the healing of a woman from
cancer through his ministry.

04 05 06 07   13 12 11 10
Printed in the United States of America

Introduction

elcome to this thirty-day journey of faith with Smith Wigglesworth. What is so intriguing about this uneducated English plumber? As I began my research, I found myself mesmerized by the original sermon notes, Bible studies and pamphlets of Smith Wigglesworth. Delightful nuggets of spiritual truths filled those brown, aging pages from the past.

This devotional series shares some of the original Smith Wigglesworth with you. I pray that your relationship with the Lord, your walk in the Spirit and your intimacy with the Father will deepen as you read afresh the words God gave a humble plumber who brought revival to his generation.

We have kept our editing of Wigglesworth to a minimum. While his language may be unpolished at times, the force and power of his expression will speak to your life.

Called a "twentieth-century apostle," Wigglesworth became a legend as God mightily used him in an evangelistic and healing ministry. Born in 1859 in Menston, Yorkshire, England, he was converted in a Wesleyan Methodist meeting at age eight and pursued a career in plumbing. He married Polly Featherstone, and he and Polly operated a little mission in Bradford, England.

In 1907, Smith Wigglesworth received the baptism of the Holy Spirit, which radically changed him and transformed his ministry into a worldwide phenomenon. Literally thousands were saved and untold scores were healed by God's power as he preached powerful messages throughout the world. He went home to the Lord he loved in 1947.

He believed that every believer could be baptized in the Holy Spirit and that God could perform miracles today as He did in the early church. Wigglesworth preached to crowds around the world and saw God perform mighty miracles, including raising the dead. He had the unusual practice of often striking, or smiting, persons with a disease. He never sought any harm to the person. He was merely expressing his anger at the devil. Wigglesworth became the forerunner of the healing ministries that emerged in the twentieth century.

As you read this booklet, take time daily in God's Word. Each devotional contains a scripture, a principle about miracles and healing from Smith Wigglesworth, and a prayer to commit that meditation to reality in your life.

I give praise to God the Father and Jesus Christ the Son for sending the Holy Spirit to inspire servants like Smith Wigglesworth to share such glorious truth and revelation so that mine and future generations might be truly blessed in Him!

Larry Keefauver, editor
1996

Far Better to Go

*For it were better for me to die,
than that any man should make
my glorying void.*
1 Corinthians 9:15

*For to me to live is Christ, and to
die is gain.*
Philippians 1:21

I believe that it is possible for God to sweep a company right into the glory before the rapture just as well as at the rapture. May God grant unto us a very keen inward discerning of our heart's purity. We want to go. It is far better for us to go, but it is far better for the church that we stay.

If you could but comprehend this word of truth that Paul spoke, "It is far better for me to go," you would never take a pill or use a plaster. You would never do anything to save yourself from going if you believed it was better to go. There is a definite, inward motion of the power of God for the human life to so change that we would not lift a finger, believing it was far better to go.

"Lord, for the purpose of being a blessing, further for Thy sake and for the sake of the church, just keep us full of life to stay."

Healing Principle #1

We would not be full of disease, but we would be full of life. Lord grant us a living faith to believe.

Pray this closing prayer today:

Jesus, going on with You is better than life itself. I desire to be filled with Thy life now and forever. Amen.

Excerpted: "Workers Together With God," Bible study no. 15, 28 July 1927, 7.

The Gift and Gifts of Healing

But the manifestation of the Spirit
is given to every man to profit
withal. For to one is given by the
Spirit the word of wisdom; to
another the word of knowledge by
the same Spirit; To another faith
by the same Spirit; to another the
gifts of healing by the same Spirit.
1 Corinthians 12:7-9

Holy Ghost people have a ministry. I pray that all the people which have received the Holy Ghost might be so filled with the Holy Ghost that, without having the gift, the Holy Ghost within them brings forth healing power.

That is the reason why I love to have people help me when I am praying for the sick. There are people who have a very dim conception of what they possess in God's Spirit.

I believe the power of the Holy Ghost which you have received has power that will bring you to a place where you dare believe for God to heal, apart from knowing that you have the gift of healing.

I deal with the gift, not gifts, of healing. There is a difference. Gifts of healing can deal with every case of sickness, every disease that there is. It is so full, beyond human expression, but you come into the fullness of it as the light of God's healing reveals it to you.

The divine gift of healing is so profound in a person with it that there is no doubt and could not be. Whatever happens would not change the man's opinion, thought or act. He expects the very thing that God intends him to have as he lays hands on the seeker.

Pray this closing prayer today:

Holy Spirit, use Your gift of healing in me.
Amen.

EXCERPTED: "Gifts of Healing," Bible study no. 16, n.d., 1.

Healed by His Word

*He sent his word, and healed them,
and delivered them from their
destructions.*

Psalm 107:20

Now there are some people here for healing; maybe some want salvation; maybe others want sanctification and the baptism of the Spirit.

Healing Principle #3

You can be healed if you will hear the Word.

This Word says it is by faith, that it might be by grace. Grace is omnipotence. It is activity, benevolence and mercy. It is truth, perfection and God's inheritance in the soul that can believe. God gives us a negative side. What is it? It is by faith. Grace is God. You open the door by faith, and God comes in with all you want. It cannot be otherwise, for it is, "of faith that it might be by grace" (Rom. 4:16). It cannot be by grace unless you say it shall be so.

This is believing, and most people want healing by feeling. It cannot be. Some even want salvation on the same line, and they say, "Oh, if I could feel I was saved, brother!" It will never come that way.

Pray this closing prayer today:

Almighty God, help me set aside my own thoughts and feelings for Thy truth. By Thy Word, not my feelings, I am healed. Hallelujah!

EXCERPTED: "Faith," Faith Booklet No. 1, n.d., 6-7.

The Spirit Manifests his Spirit in Us

But the manifestation of the Spirit is
given to every man to profit withal.
1 Corinthians 12:7

God has privileged us in Christ Jesus to live above the ordinary human plane of life. Those who want to be "ordinary" and live on a lower plane, can do so; but as for me, I will not!

Healing Principle #4

The same unction, the same zeal, the same Holy Ghost power is at our command as it was at the command of Stephen and the apostles.

We have the same God that Abraham and Elijah had. We need not come behind in any gift or grace. We may not possess the abiding gifts, but if we are full of the Holy Ghost and divine unction it is possible, when there is need, for God to manifest every gift of the Spirit through us or to give a manifestation of the gifts as God may choose to use us.

This *ordinary* man Stephen became mighty under the Holy Ghost's anointing. He stands supreme, in many ways, among the apostles. "And Stephen, full of faith and power, did great wonders and miracles among the people" (Acts 6:8). Stephen was just as ordinary a man as you and me, but he was in the place where God could so move upon him that he, in turn, could move all before him. He began in a most humble place and ended in a blaze of glory. Beloved, *dare to believe in Christ!*

Pray this closing prayer today:

Holy Spirit, empower me to go beyond the ordinary to the extraordinary through Thy power and unction. Amen.

EXCERPTED: "Extraordinary," Faith Booklet No. 2, n.d., 3-4.

Healing Without Laying On Hands

And as many as touched him
[Jesus] were made whole.
Mark 6:56

When I went to Sweden, they would not let me lay hands on people for healing. I know God is not subject to my laying hands upon people in order for them to be healed.

Healing Principle #5

When the presence of the Lord is
there to heal, it does not require
hands. Faith is the great opera-
tion position. When we believe
God, all things are easy.

So they built places where I could speak to thousands of people in Sweden. I prayed. "Lord, you know. You have never been yet in any place fixed. You have the mind of all things; show me how it can be done today without the people having hands laid upon them. Show me."

To all the people I said, "All of you that would like the power of God going through you today, healing everything, put your hands up."

Thousands of hands went up. "Lord, show me." And He told me as clearly as anything to pick a person out that stood upon a rock. It was a very rocky place. So I told them all to put their hands down but this person. To her I said, "Tell all the people your troubles." She began to relate her troubles from her head to her feet. She was in so much pain.

"Lift your hands high," I said. "In the name of Jesus, I rebuke the evil one from your head to your feet. I believe He has loosed you."

Oh, how she danced and jumped and shouted! That was the first time God revealed to me it could be done. Hundreds were healed without a touch and hundreds saved with touching. Our God is a God of mighty power.

Pray this closing prayer today:

Lord, I need no touch but Thine to heal me. If Thou but touch me, Lord, I will be healed. Amen.

EXCERPTED: "Workers Together With God," Bible study no. 15, 28 July 1927, 13.

Salvation and Healing

*When Jesus saw their faith, he said
unto the sick of the palsy, Son, thy
sins be forgiven thee...But that ye
may know that the Son of man
hath power on earth to forgive
sins...I say unto thee, Arise, and
take up thy bed, and go thy way
into thine house.*

Mark 2:5,10-11

Before leaving home, I received a wire telling me that I should go to Liverpool. There was a woman with cancer and gall stones who was down with much discouragement. If I know God is sending me, my faith rises. God sent me to her.

The woman said, "I have no hope."

"Well," I said, "I have not come from Bradford to go back home with a bad report."

God said to me, "Establish her in the fact of

the new birth." When she had the assurance that her sin was gone and she was born again, she said, "That [salvation] is everything to me. Cancer is nothing now. I have Jesus!"

The battle was won. God delivered her. She was free from sin and disease. She got up, dressed and was happy in Jesus.

Healing Principle #6

When God speaks, it is as a nail in a sure place.

Will you believe?

Pray this closing prayer today:

Jesus, You are my salvation and my healing. I believe that You alone can set me free from sin and sickness. Amen.

EXCERPTED: "Now! Now! Now!," message presented in Colombier, Switzerland, n.d., 5.

Filled With the Spirit

And be not drunk with wine,
wherein is excess; but be filled
with the Spirit.
Ephesians 5:18

There is a necessity for every one of us to be filled with God. It is not sufficient to have just a "touch," or to be filled with a "desire." The only thing that will meet the needs of the people is for you to be immersed in God so that whether you eat or drink, or whatever you do, it may be all for the glory of God. In that place you will find that all your strength, mind and soul is filled with a zeal, not only for worship, but for proclamation.

That proclamation will be accompanied by all the power of God, which must move Satanic power, disturb the world and make it feel upset.

The reason the world is not see-ing Jesus is because Christian people are not filled with Jesus

They are satisfied with weekly meetings, occasionally reading the Bible and sometimes praying. Beloved, if God lays hold of you by the Spirit, you will find that there is an end of everything and a beginning of God so that your whole body becomes seasoned with a divine likeness of God.

Pray this closing prayer today:

Fill me, Holy Spirit. May those people with whom I come into contact daily see only Jesus when they look at my life. Make me a divine likeness of God. Amen.

EXCERPTED: "Divine Life Brings Divine Health," pamphlet (North Melbourne, Australia: Victory Press, n.d.), 1.

Healed by God's Resurrection Touch

*Then Peter said, Silver and gold
have I none; but such as I have give
I thee: In the name of Jesus Christ
of Nazareth rise up and walk.
And he took him by the right hand,
and lifted him up: and
immediately his feet and ankle
bones received strength.*
Acts 3:6-7

man who had spent years in a wheelchair but who had been healed, came on the platform and told how he was loosed. Another person with a blood issue for many years testified. A blind man told how he got his eyes opened.

I said to the people, "Are you ready?" Oh, they were so ready. A dear man got hold of a boy who was encased in iron from top to bottom, lifted him up and placed him on the platform. Hands were laid upon him in the name of Jesus.

"Papa! Papa! Papa!" he said. "It's all over me! O Papa, come take these irons off!" And the father took the irons off. Healing had gone all over the boy.

This is what I feel. The life of God is going all over me, the power of God is all over me

Healing Principle #8

Don't you know this resurrection touch, this divine life? This is what God has brought us into.

Let it go over us, Lord, the power of the Holy Ghost, the resurrection of heaven, the sweetness of His benediction and the joy of the Lord!

Pray this closing prayer today:

Touch me, Lord, with Thy resurrection power, Thy blessing and Thy joy. Amen.

EXCERPTED: "Ephesians 4:1-16," Bible study no. 9, 19 July 1927, 5-6.

Casting
Out Devils

*For he [Jesus] said unto him, Come
out of the man, thou unclean spirit.
And he asked him, What is thy
name? And he answered, saying, My
name is Legion: for we are many...
And all the devils besought him, saying, Send us into the swine, that we
may enter into them. And forthwith
Jesus gave them leave.*
Mark 5:8-9,12-13

After many calls, letters and requests, I went
to London. When I got there, the dear father
and mother of the needy one took my hands,
led me up onto a balcony and pointed to a
door that was open a little. I went in that door
and have never seen a sight like it in my life.

I saw a young woman, beautiful to look at,
but she had four big men holding her down to
the floor. Her clothing was torn from the strug-

gle. Her eyes rolled, and she could not speak. She was exactly like that man who saw Jesus and ran out from the tombs. As soon as he got to Jesus, he couldn't speak, but the demon power spoke and said, "I know you. You can't cast us out. We are many."

"Yes," I said, "I know you are many, but my Lord Jesus will cast you all out." The power of Satan was so great upon this beautiful girl that she whirled and broke away from the four strong men.

The Spirit of the Lord was wonderful in me, and I went right up to her, looked into her face, seeing the evil powers there.

Healing Principle #9

Her very eyes flashed with demon power. "In the name of Jesus," I said, "I command you to leave. Though you are many, I command you to leave this moment in the name of Jesus."

She instantly became sick and vomited out thirty-seven evil spirits, giving them a name as they came out. That day she was made as perfect as anybody. The next morning at ten o'clock, I sat at the table with her and had breaking of bread. Praise the Lord!

Pray this closing prayer today:

At the name of Jesus, every demon must flee. Amen.

EXCERPTED: Bible study no. 8, 15 July 1927, 15-16.

It Is
Finished

When Jesus therefore had received
the vinegar, he said, It is finished:
and he bowed his head, and
gave up the ghost.

John 19:30

When I was in Cazadero seven or eight years ago, amongst the first people that came to me in those meetings was a man who was stone deaf. Every time we had a meeting, as I rose to speak this man would take his chair from the ordinary row and place it right in front of me. The devil used to say, "Now you're done."

I said, "No, I am not done. It is finished." After the meeting had been going on for three weeks, one night as we were singing this man became tremendously disturbed. He looked in every direction. He became as one that had almost lost his mind.

Then he took a leap. He started on the run and went out amongst the people. He went out about sixty yards away and heard singing. The Lord said, "Thy ears are open."

The man came back, and we were still singing. That stopped our singing. He told us that when his ears were opened, there was such a tremendous noise, he could not understand what it was. He thought something had happened to the world. He ran out of the meeting. As he got outside, he heard the singing.

Healing Principle #10

Oh, the devil said for three weeks, "You cannot do it." I said, "It is done."

As though God would ever forget! As though God could forget! As if it were possible for God to ignore our prayers!

Pray this closing prayer today:

Lord, by faith we claim Your completed, miraculous work in our lives. It is finished! Amen.

EXCERPTED: "Faith (Part One)," message presented at Glad Tidings Tabernacle, 2 August 1922, 5.

Hindering Evil Spirits

Beloved, believe not every spirit, but try the spirits whether they are of God: because many false prophets are gone out into the world.

1 John 4:1

One day I met a friend of mine in the street and I said, "Fred, where are you going?"

"I am going...Oh, I don't feel I ought to tell you," he said. "It is a secret between God and me."

"Now we have prayed together. We have had nights of communication. We have been living in the Spirit," I said. "Surely there is no secret that could be hid from me by you."

"I'm going to a spiritualistic meeting," he said.

"Don't you think that's dangerous?" I asked.

"No," he said. "They are having some special mediums from London." He meant to say they were having some people from London more filled with the devil than we had in

Bradford. They were special devils.

"I am going," he said, "with the clear knowledge that I am under the blood."

"Tell me the results," I requested. He agreed.

Later he told me that the séance had begun, the lights went low and everything was dismal.

Healing Principle #11

The mediums had tried every possible thing they could for over an hour to get under control. Then the light went up and they said, "We can do nothing tonight. Some here believe in the blood."

Pray this closing prayer today:

A million thanks, Lord, for the blood of Jesus. Cover me, my family and all around me with the powerful blood of Jesus. Amen.

EXCERPTED: "Testing of Spirits," Bible study no. 10, 20 July 1927, 5-6.

Our Chief Executive —The Holy Spirit

*But the Comforter, which is the Holy
Ghost, whom the Father will send in
my name, he shall teach you all
things, and bring all things to your
remembrance, whatsoever I have
said unto you.*

John 14:26

A chief executive is one who has a right to
declare everything on the board. The chief
executive in the world is the Holy Ghost. He
is here today as a communicant to our hearts,
to our minds, to our thoughts, saying whatever God wants us to know.

So this Holy Executive in us can speak wonderful words. The Spirit will teach you, bring
all things to your remembrance. You need not
have any man teach you, but the unction
abideth and you need no teachers.

Smith Wigglesworth ✺ 27

Healing Principle #12

You need the Teacher, which is the Holy Spirit, to bring all things to your remembrance.

This is the office of the Holy Spirit. This is the power of His communication. This is what Paul means when he says, "God is love." Jesus, who is grace, is with you. But the Holy Ghost is the speaker. He speaks everything concerning Jesus.

Pray this closing prayer today:

Holy Spirit, speak to me. Teach me that I may know, understand and apply the Word. Amen.

EXCERPTED: "Testing of Spirits," Bible study no. 10, 20 July 1927, 8-9.

Fullness of the Spirit —his Baptism, his Best!

For John truly baptized with water; but ye shall be baptized with the Holy Ghost not many days hence.

Acts 1:5

There are three things in life, and I notice that many people are satisfied with only one. There is blessing in justification; in sanctification; and in the baptism of the Holy Spirit.

Salvation is a wonderful thing, and we know it. Sanctification is a process that takes you on to a higher height with God. Salvation, sanctification and the fullness of the Spirit are processes

Healing Principle #13

Any number of people are satisfied with "good" — that is

justification or salvation. Other people are satisfied with "better" — that is a sanctified life, purified by God. Other people are satisfied with the "best" — that is the fulless of God with revelation from on high.

So I come to you with the fullness of God in the Holy Spirit through His baptism. I come not with good, but better; not with better, but with best. Continue to grow and improve spiritually. Keep going on with God.

Pray this closing prayer today:

Heavenly Father, I thank Thee for the goodness of Thy salvation and the going on with Thee through sanctification, the baptism of Thy Spirit and the fullness of Thee in my total being. Amen.

EXCERPTED: "Temptation Endured," Bible study no. 12, 22 July 1927, 12.

Sanctified
by the Spirit

*Elect according to the foreknowl-
edge of God the Father, through
sanctification of the Spirit, unto
obedience and sprinkling of the
blood of Jesus Christ: Grace unto
you, and peace, be multiplied.*
                                    1 Peter 1:2

There is a sanctifying of the human spirit.
It does not matter what you say, if your
human spirit does not get wholly sanctified,
you will always be in danger. It is that position
where the devil has a chance to work on you.

Therefore, we are taught to come into sanctification, where the rudiments, the uncleanness,
the inordinate affections and corruptions pass
away because of incorruption abiding. In sanctification, all kinds of lusts have lost their power.

This is the plan. Only in the ideal pursuit of
this, does God so bless us in our purifying

Smith Wigglesworth ❈ 31

state that we lose our earthly position and ascend with Him in glory. The saints of God, as they go on into perfection and holiness, understanding the mind of the Spirit and the law of the Spirit of life, are brought into a very blessed place — the place of holiness, the place of entire sanctification, the place where God is enthroned in the heart.

Healing Principle #14

The sanctified mind is so concentrated in the power of God that the saint thinks about the things that are pure and lives in holy ascendancy, where every day he experiences the power and liberty of God.

God highly honors him — but He never exalts him. The devil comes to exalt him, but it cannot be under the lines of the sanctification of the Spirit. There is a sanctifying of the human spirit where the human spirit so comes into perfect blending with the divine mind of Christ that the saint does not desire to be exalted. The Spirit can sanctify your spirit until you will never vaunt yourself and will never say "I...I...I," but it will be, "Christ, Christ, Christ!" He, not "I," will be glorified.

Pray this closing prayer today:

Sanctify me, Holy Spirit, that I may be filled with Thee, not me. Amen.

EXCERPTED: "The Glory of the Incorruptible," Bible study no. 13, 26 July 1927, 5-6.

Healed By his Stripes

But he was wounded for our transgressions, he was bruised for our iniquities: the chastisement of our peace was upon him; and with his stripes we are healed.

Isaiah 53:5

I went to visit a sick woman whose address was given to me in Belfast. At her house, a young man met me at the door and pointed me to go up the stairway. When I got up onto the landing, there was a door wide open, so I walked right into the doorway and found a woman sitting up on the bed. As soon as I looked at her, I knew she couldn't speak to me, so I began to pray.

Healing Principle #15

She was moving backwards and

forwards, gasping for breath.
When I prayed the Lord said to
me, "Read Isaiah 53." When I got
to the fifth verse, the woman
shouted, "I am healed!"

"Oh," I said, "woman tell me."

She said, "Three weeks ago I was cleaning the house. I moved some furniture, strained my heart and moved it out of its place. The doctors examined me and said I would die of suffocation. But last night, in the middle of the night, I saw you come into my room. When you saw me you knew I couldn't speak, so you began to pray. Then you opened to Isaiah 53 and read until you came to the fifth verse. When you read the fifth verse, I was completely healed. That was a vision. Now it is a fact."

I know that the Word of God is true!

Pray this closing prayer today:

Jesus, by Your stripes I am healed. Amen.

Excerpted: "Praying for the Sick," sermon on divine healing, 6 July 1927, 11.

The Holy Spirit Quickens

*But if the Spirit of him that raised
up Jesus from the dead dwell in
you, he that raised up Christ from
the dead shall also quicken your
mortal bodies by his Spirit that
dwelleth in you.*

Romans 8:11

Many people are receiving a clear knowledge of an inward working power from the
Spirit which is not only quickening their
mortal bodies, but also pressing into that natural body an incorruptible power which is
manifesting itself, getting ready for the rapture.

It is the inward life, the new man in the old
man, the new nature in the old nature, the resurrection power in the dead form, the quickening of all, the divine order of God manifested in the human body that quickens us, giving

us life. The nature of the living Christ gives us power over all death.

Healing Principle #16

Do not be afraid to claim the quickening, life-giving power of the Holy Spirit. That is power over all sin, power over all disease.

The life of Christ is at work in your body to form and quicken until every vestige of the natural order is eaten up by the Life Divine.

The former law was of the natural man. Now the new law is of the life of the Spirit or the manifestation of the new creation, which is Christ in us, the manifested power of the Glory. Glory is a manifestation of a Divine nature in the human body.

Pray this closing prayer today:

Holy Spirit, quicken my body with thy divine nature and glory. Amen.

EXCERPTED: "This Grace," Bible study no. 26, 19 August 1927, 2.

Why Wait on the Holy Spirit?

*But wait for the promise of the
Father, which, saith he, ye have
heard of me. For John truly
baptized with water; but ye shall be
baptized with the Holy Ghost not
many days hence.*

Acts 1:4-5

The disciples tarried at Jerusalem till they were endued with power from on high. We know that the Holy Ghost came. It was right for them to tarry. It is wrong now to wait for the Holy Ghost to come. He has come!

Then why are we waiting? Why do we not all receive the Holy Ghost? Because our bodies are not ready for it. Our temples are not cleansed. When our temples are purified and our minds put in order, then the Holy Ghost can take full charge. The Holy Ghost is not a manifestation of carnality.

The Holy Ghost is most lovely. He is the great refiner. He is full of divine, not natural life. Don't wait. I desire for you to lift your minds, elevate your thoughts, come out of the world into a place where you know that you have rest for your feet.

Healing Principle #17

Cease from your own works so that God can work mightily in you to will and to do His good pleasure.

Desire the inrushing river of the Holy Ghost — a pure, holy and divine river of living water to flow through you. Not later. Now!

Pray this closing prayer today:

Holy Spirit, purify my heart, my life. Flow in me and through me, now. Amen.

EXCERPTED: A teaching on John 7:37-39, n.d., 3.

Divine Healing

Bless the Lord, O my soul, and forget not all his benefits: Who forgiveth all thine iniquities; Who healeth all thy diseases.
Psalm 103:2-3

The gift of divine healing is more than audacity, more than unction. People sometimes come to me very troubled. They will say, "I had the gift of healing once, but something has happened, and I do not have it now."

You never had it. "Gifts and calling of God are without repentance" (Rom. 11:29). If you fall from grace and use a gift wrongly, it will work against you. If you use tongues out of the will of God, interpretation will condemn you. If you have been used and the gift has been exercised and you have fallen from your high place, it will work against you.

The gift of the Holy Spirit, when He has breathed in you, will make you alive so that it is wonderful.

It seems almost then as though you have never been born. The jealousy God has over us, the interest He has in us, the purpose He has for us, the grandeur of His glory are so marvelous. God has called us into this place to receive gifts.

Pray this closing prayer today:

Lord, thank You for the wonderful sense of life that has been given to me through Your Holy Spirit. I seek to be used by Your Holy Spirit that I might use Your gifts for Your glory. Amen.

EXCERPTED: "Gifts of Healing," Bible study no. 16, n.d., 3.

The Spirit in You

*And I [Jesus] will pray the Father,
and he shall give you another
Comforter, that he may abide with
you for ever.*

John 14:16

There is a difference between the Spirit being *in* you and the Spirit being *with* you. For instance, we are getting light now from outside this building. This is exactly the position of every believer that is not baptized with the Holy Ghost. The Spirit is with every person that is not baptized, and they have light from the outside. But suppose all the light that is coming through the window was inside.

That is exactly what is to be taking place. We have revelation from outside, revelation in many ways by the Spirit, but after He comes inside, it is revelation from inside which will make things outside right.

We are baptizing people in water, remembering that they are put to death, because every believer ought to be covered. Every believer must be put to death in water baptism.

The baptism of the Spirit is to be planted deeper until there is not a part of you that is left. There is a manifestation of the power of the new creation by the Holy Spirit right in our mortal bodies.

Healing Principle #19

Where once we were, now He reigns supreme, manifesting the very Christ inside of us, the Holy Ghost fulfilling all things right there.

Pray this closing prayer today:

Spirit of God, go with me and immerse me with Thy living water that You might reign in all of me. Amen.

EXCERPTED: "Ephesians 4:1-16," Bible study no. 9, 19 July 1927, 7-8.

Faith
and Healing

*But Jesus turned him about, and
when he saw her, he said,
Daughter, be of good comfort; thy
faith hath made thee whole. And
the woman was made whole from
that hour.*

Matthew 9:22

I believe that we ought to have people
loosed from their infirmities without being
touched. I more and more see that day in
which the Lord's visitation is upon us so that
the presence of the Lord is here to heal. We
should have people healed in meetings in
which I speak while they are under the unction of the Holy Spirit.

I have been preaching faith so that you may
definitely claim your healing. I believe if you
listen to the Word and are moved to believe,
and if you stand up while I pray, you will find

healing virtue loosed in you.

Healing Principle #20

God wants you to have a living faith now, to get a vital touch from Him, shaking the foundation of all weakness.

When you were saved, you were saved the moment you believed. You will be healed the moment you believe.

Pray this closing prayer today:

Lord, I desire a touch from You that will shake the foundation of all my weakness. Grant me the faith to receive the healing You have for me in Jesus' mighty name. Amen.

EXCERPTED: "Praying for the Sick," sermon on divine healing, 6 July 1927, 13.

Holy Spirit—Wind, Person and Fire

*He that believeth on me, as the
scripture hath said, out of his belly
shall flow rivers of living water.
(But this spake he of the Spirit,
which they that believe on him
should receive: for the Holy Ghost
was not yet given; because that
Jesus was not yet glorified.)*
John 7:38-39

Jesus spoke about the Holy Ghost which
was to be given. In Acts 2 we find three man-
ifestations of the Holy Ghost — wind, person
and fire. The first manifestation is a rushing
mighty wind. Second, there are cloven
tongues of fire. Think of the mighty wind and
the cloven tongues of fire over everyone.
Third, see the incoming and outflowing of the
Holy Ghost.

Can we be filled with this river? How is it

possible for us to flow a river?

Healing Principle #21

A river of water is always an emblem of the Word of God, the Water of life, and so when the Holy Ghost comes, He clothes and anoints the Christ who is already indwelling the believer.

You will never get to know God better by testimony. Testimony should always come through the Word. You will not get to know God better by prayer. Prayer has to come out of the Word. The Word is the only thing that reveals God and is going to be helpful in the world. When the breath and the presence of God comes, the Holy Spirit speaks expressively according to the mind of the Father and the Son.

So when you are filled with the person of the Holy Ghost, then the breath, the power, the unction, the fire of the Spirit takes hold of the Word of Life, which is Christ. God wants to fill you with that divine power so that out of you will flow living waters.

Pray this closing prayer today:

Oh fire, wind and person of the Holy Spirit, out of me flow living waters that others might know Jesus through me. Amen.

Excerpted: A teaching on John 7:37-39, n.d., 3-4.

God Doesn't Bring Disease

God be merciful unto us, and bless us; and cause his face to shine upon us; Selah. That thy way may be known upon earth, thy saving health among all nations.

Psalm 67:1-2

Some people talk about God being pleased to put disease on His children. "Here is a person I love," says God. "I will break his arm. In order that he should love me more, I will break his leg. In order that he should love me still more, I will give him a weak heart. And in order to increase that love, I will make him so that he cannot eat anything without having indigestion."

The whole thing won't stand daylight. Is it right now to say, "You know, my brother, I have suffered so much in this affliction that it has made me know God better"? Well, now, before you get up, ask God for a lot more affliction, so you will get to know Him better still. If you won't ask for more affliction to make you purer still, I won't believe that the first affliction made you purer; because if it had, you would have more faith in it. It appears you haven't faith in your afflictions. It is only language, but language doesn't count unless it works out a fact. But if the people can see that your language is working out a fact, then they have some grounds for believing in it.

Healing Principle #22

I have looked through my Bible, and I cannot find where God brings disease and sickness.

It isn't God at all, but the devil that brings sickness and disease.

Pray this closing prayer today:

In Jesus' name, I rebuke disease and sick-ness. Lord God, You are the Great Physician. I declare healing in Your mighty name.
Amen.

EXCERPTED: "Christ in Us," pamphlet (North Melbourne, Australia: Victory Press, n.d.), 9-10.

Walk and Live in the Spirit

That the righteousness of the law might be fulfilled in us, who walk not after the flesh, but after the Spirit.

Romans 8:4

We must know that the baptism of the Spirit immerses us into an intensity of zeal, into a likeness to Jesus, to make us into pure, running metal, so hot for God that it travels like oil from vessel to vessel.

This divine line of the Spirit will let us see where we have ceased and He has begun. We are at the end for a beginning. We are down and out, and God is in and out.

There isn't a natural thought of any use here. There isn't a thing that is carnal, earthly, natural, that can ever live in a meeting.

No man is able to walk spiritually without being in the Spirit. He must live in the Spirit.

He must realize all the time that he is growing in the same ideal of his Master, in season and out of season, always beholding the face of the Master, Jesus.

Pray this closing prayer today:

Holy Spirit, immerse me that Thy zeal will run hot in my life for Jesus Christ. May I never stop growing more and more Christlike through Your power. Amen.

EXCERPTED: "Ye Are Our Epistle (Part One)," message presented at Glad Tidings Tabernacle, 23 August 1922, 4.

The Spirit Reveals the Son

*And hope maketh not ashamed;
because the love of God is shed
abroad in our hearts by the Holy
Ghost which is given unto us.*
Romans 5:5

The love of God is shed abroad in our hearts by the Holy Ghost. The manifestation of the revelation of God's Son by the Holy Ghost comes by the Holy Spirit who is revealing Him to us as so uniquely divine that He is in power of overcoming, in power of purity, in power of rising all the time.

The Holy Ghost is shed abroad in our hearts for the very purpose that we may know that the inner man in us has to go on to develop — it must not cease growing. The Holy Ghost in us creates development and empowers us to move out as the Lord would have us be.

Healing Principle #24

The Spirit lifts. The Word of incarnation moves. The Life Divine operates. The Spirit quickeneth.

You are being changed, made right, made ready, changed by regenerating.

The Lord's life is moving and flowing. Put thy spirit into the joy of the breath of God. Let yourself go on the bosom of His love. Be transformed by all the Spirit's life from above.

Pray this closing prayer today:

Holy Spirit, grow the image of Christ in me that I might reveal His love in my life. Change me and make me ready to be your servant through the transformation of your presence in my life. Amen.

EXCERPTED: "This Grace," Bible study no. 26, 19 August 1927, 5-6.

The Life of the Spirit

*And Joshua...and Caleb...spake
unto all the company of the
children of Israel, saying, The
land...is an exceeding good
land....a land which floweth with
milk and honey. Only rebel not ye
against the Lord, neither fear ye the
people of the land; for they are
bread for us: their defence is
departed from them, and the Lord
is with us: fear them not.*
Numbers 14:6-9

The Spirit was so mighty upon Joshua and Caleb that they had no fear. The Holy Spirit upon them had such a dignity of reverence to God that these two people brought the bunches of grapes and presented them to the people. There were ten people sent out. They had not the Holy Spirit and came back murmuring.

Smith Wigglesworth ❀ 53

If you get filled with the Spirit, you will never murmur again.

I am speaking about people who get the Holy Ghost and go on with God, not about the people who remain stationery.

I pray that the same Holy Spirit on Joshua and Caleb will fill you and search your hearts. Be filled with the life of the Spirit that we call unction, revelation and force. What do I call force? Force is that position in the power of the Spirit where, instead of wavering, you go through. Instead of judgment, you receive truth.

Pray this closing prayer today:

Holy Spirit, fill me with Thy boldness and power to go on with Thee and not to waver or murmur. Amen.

EXCERPTED: "Possession of the Rest," message presented in Wellington, New Zealand, 14 January 1924, 3.

Full of Faith and the Holy Spirit

*And the saying pleased the whole
multitude: and they chose Stephen,
a man full of faith and of
the Holy Ghost.*

Acts 6:5

Something happened in the life of this man [Stephen], chosen for menial service, and he became mighty for God. Faithful in little, God brought him to full fruition. Under the inspiration of divine power by which he spoke, they could not help but listen — even the angels listened.

As I read about Stephen in Acts 6 and 7, I have a vision of this scene in every detail — the howling mob with their vengeful, murderous spirits ready to devour this holy man; and he, "being full of the Holy Ghost," gazing steadfastly into heaven. From his place of helplessness, he looked up and said, "Behold,

I see the heavens opened, and the Son of man standing at the right hand of God."

Is that the position that Jesus went to take? No!

Healing Principle #26

He went to sit at the right hand of the Father; but in behalf of the "first martyr," in behalf of the man with that burning flame of Holy Ghost power, God's Son stood up in honorary testimony of him who, called to serve tables, was faithful unto death.

This man chosen for an ordinary task but filled with the Holy Ghost was so moved upon by God that he finished his earthly work in a blaze of glory, magnifying God with his last breath. Looking up into the face of the Master, he said, "Lord Jesus, forgive them! Lay not this sin to their charge!" And when he had said thus, he fell asleep. Friends, it is worth all to gain that spirit. What a divine ending to the life and testimony of a man that was "chosen to serve tables."

Pray this closing prayer today:

Lord Jesus, fill me with faith and the Holy Spirit, that I might blaze with Thy glory like Stephen no matter what I face in life. Amen.

EXCERPTED: "Extraordinary," Faith Booklet No. 2, n.d., 4-5.

Our Inheritance Sealed in the Spirit

In whom [Christ] also we have obtained an inheritance, being predestinated according to the purpose of him who worketh all things after the counsel of his own will: That we should be to the praise of his glory, who first trusted in Christ. In whom ye also trusted, after that ye heard the word of truth, the gospel of your salvation: in whom also after that ye believed, ye were sealed with that holy Spirit of promise.
Ephesians 1:11-13

God says you are not of this world; you have been delivered from the corruption of the world; you are being transformed by the renewing of your mind. God says that you are a royal priesthood, a holy people, belonging to the building and Christ is the great cornerstone.

The Holy Spirit is coming forth to help you claim your inheritance. Do not be afraid of getting rich or of coming in, but be very afraid if you do not come in. Have God's mind on this. God says you have to overcome the world; you must have this incorruptible, unde-filed position now within the human body, transforming your mind, even your very nature.

Healing Principle #27

Realize that the supernatural power of God is working through you by His Spirit.

The glorious incarnation of the Spirit is our inheritance. This is where God wants to make you His own in such a way that you will deny yourself, the flesh and the world. You can reign in this life by this lovely place, this inher-itance in Christ Jesus sealed by the Holy Spirit.

Pray this closing prayer today:

Holy Spirit, seal me in Thy inheritance of glory through the precious name of Jesus. Amen.

EXCERPTED: "The Glory of the Incorruptible," Bible study no. 13, 26 July 1927, 10.

Intoxicated by the Spirit

*And be not drunk with wine,
wherein is excess; but be filled
with the Spirit.*
Ephesians 5:18

When you are intoxicated with the Spirit, the Spirit life flows through the avenues of your mind and the deep perception of the heart with deep throbbings.

Healing Principle #28

You are so filled with the passion of the grace of God, that you are illumined by the power of new wine — the wine of the kingdom, the Holy Ghost — till your whole body is intoxicated.

This is rapture! There is no natural body that

can stand the process of this going forth. It will have to leave the body at His coming. But the body will be a preserver to it until the sons of God are marvelously manifested.

This holy new life, this preservative of the Son of God in your human body, this life in you is so after the order of God that it is not ashamed in any way to say you are coming into co-equality with the Father, with the Son and with the Holy Spirit.

Pray this closing prayer today:

Thank You for allowing my life to be filled with the preservative of Your Son's presence within my human body.
Fill and intoxicate me, O Holy Spirit, that I might live and move in Thee. Amen.

EXCERPTED: "This Grace," Bible study no. 26, 19 August 1927, 11.

Is Healing the Main Thing?

*But seek ye first the kingdom
of God, and his righteousness;
and all these things shall be
added unto you.*

Matthew 6:33

Jesus came to make us free from sin — free from disease and pain. When I see a person diseased and in pain, I have great compassion for them, and when I lay my hands upon them, I know God means for men to be so filled with Him that the power of sin shall have no effect upon them. They shall go forth, as I am doing, to help the needy, sick and afflicted.

Healing Principle #29

But what is the main thing? To preach the kingdom of God and His righteousness.

Jesus came to do this. John came preaching repentance. The disciples began by preaching repentance toward God and faith in the Lord Jesus Christ.

I tell you, beloved, if you have really been changed by God, there is a repentance in your heart never to be repented of.

Through the revelation of the Word of God, we find that divine healing is solely for the glory of God and salvation is to make you to know you now have to be inhabited by another, even God, and you have to walk with God in newness of life.

Pray this closing prayer today:

Jesus, Thou art the One who not only saves the body, but Thou hast saved my soul and spirit. Wholeness is found only in Thee.
Amen.

EXCERPTED: "Divine Life Brings Divine Health," pamphlet (North Melbourne, Australia: Victory Press, n.d.), 8.

Unity in the Spirit

*Endeavoring to keep the unity of the
Spirit in the bond of peace.*
Ephesians 4:3

Beloved, I want you to remember that the church is one body. She has many members, but we are all members of that one body. At any cost, we must keep the body in perfect unity.

Healing Principle #30

Never try to get the applause of people by a natural thing. Yours has to be a spiritual breath. Your word has to be the Word of God.

As the church is bound together in one Spirit, the people of the church have one voice, one desire and one plan. When the church has the mind of the Spirit with Christ, nothing can then break the church.

Holy Spirit, make me a force and power for Thy unity within the Body of Christ. Amen.

EXCERPTED: "Our Calling (Part One)," message presented at Glad Tidings Tabernacle, 18 August 1922, 5.

The Wigglesworth Series

The following thirty-day devotionals
are also available.

Smith Wigglesworth on Prayer

Smith Wigglesworth never read any other
book than the Bible. He viewed prayer
as an act of faith that claimed the truth
of God's Word as a sure foundation for
victory in all of life's trials. Discover
timeless insights into God's Word and
prayer as you use this devotional.

Smith Wigglesworth on Faith

Smith Wigglesworth often challenged his
listeners by saying, "Faith is an act. Faith is
a leap. Faith jumps in. Faith claims. Faith's
author is Jesus." Let his perspective on
faith challenge you as you read this thirty-
day devotional.

Available at your local Christian
bookstore or from:

Charisma House
600 Rinehart Road
Lake Mary, FL 32746
1-800-599-5750